Rapping about
The air around us

Bobbie Kalman
Crabtree Publishing Company

www.crabtreebooks.com

Created by Bobbie Kalman

For Emma and Quinn Fletcher, twin soul sisters
There is something special in the air
when you two are around.

Author and Editor-in-Chief
Bobbie Kalman

Editors
Kathy Middleton
Crystal Sikkens

Photo research
Bobbie Kalman

Design
Bobbie Kalman
Katherine Berti
Samantha Crabtree
  (logo and front cover)

Print and production coordinator
Katherine Berti

Prepress technician
Katherine Berti

Illustrations
Bonna Rouse: page 21

Photographs
iStockphoto: page 14
Nonthaburi, Thailand-October 20:
  Rufous/Shutterstock: page 19
  (bottom left)
All other images by Shutterstock

Library and Archives Canada Cataloguing in Publication

Kalman, Bobbie
    Rapping about the air around us / Bobbie Kalman.

(Rapping about--)
Includes index.
Issued also in electronic formats.
ISBN 978-0-7787-2797-2 (bound).--ISBN 978-0-7787-2804-7 (pbk.)

1. Air--Juvenile literature. I. Title. II. Series: Rapping about--

QC161.2.K357 2012   j533'.6   C2012-900676-9

Library of Congress Cataloging-in-Publication Data

CIP available at Library of Congress

Crabtree Publishing Company

www.crabtreebooks.com   1-800-387-7650

Printed in Canada/022012/AV20120110

Published in Canada
Crabtree Publishing
616 Welland Ave.
St. Catharines, Ontario
L2M 5V6

Published in the United States
Crabtree Publishing
PMB 59051
350 Fifth Avenue, 59th Floor
New York, New York 10118

Published in the United Kingdom
Crabtree Publishing
Maritime House
Basin Road North, Hove
BN41 1WR

Published in Australia
Crabtree Publishing
3 Charles Street
Coburg North
VIC 3058

Contents

Air on Earth

Earth is surrounded by layers of **gases** that make up the **atmosphere**. The atmosphere is like a blanket of air allowing us to live here. It protects us from the rays of the sun so we can play outdoors and have fun.

atmosphere

Staying alive

The atmosphere contains the air we breathe.

Without it, we could not survive.

Each minute we take ten breaths or more.

Each breath we take keeps us alive.

Animals also need to breathe air—

from ladybugs to a big brown bear.

Plants use air in a different way.

Read page 14 to

learn how today.

ladybugs

brown
bear

plant leaf

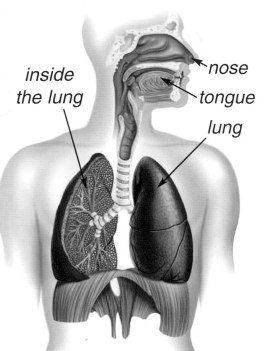

inside the lung

nose

tongue

lung

Breathing air

Oxygen is the part of air we need.

We **inhale** this gas when we breathe.

Carbon dioxide is the gas we **exhale**.

We do this with each breath, without fail.

We inhale air with our noses and **lungs**.

We blow air out past our lips and tongues.

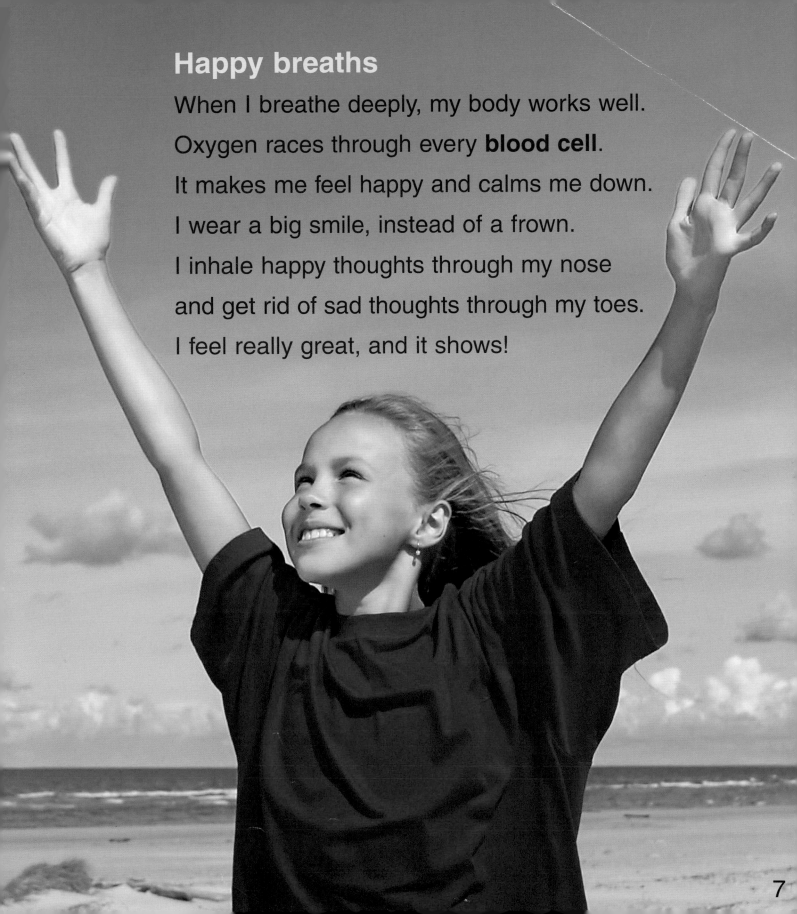

Happy breaths

When I breathe deeply, my body works well.

Oxygen races through every **blood cell**.

It makes me feel happy and calms me down.

I wear a big smile, instead of a frown.

I inhale happy thoughts through my nose

and get rid of sad thoughts through my toes.

I feel really great, and it shows!

Air and water

Air contains **water vapor** that rises,

The vapor creates clouds of all sizes.

When the clouds have more water than they can contain,

water falls from them as hail, snow, or rain.

Air is also in the water
of a lake, river, or sea.
Where can the air
in this ocean be?

air bubbles

Breathing water, too

Our breath contains several gases.

It contains water vapor, too.

When we exhale vapor from our mouths,

it becomes clouds, rain, and **dew**. ⟶

It does not stop moving or changing.

Water is in the breath you just drew!

water vapor

Breathing in water

Most animals that live in water breathe air through **organs** called **gills**. Some gills look like tiny slits, and some look more like frills.

gill slits

These gills look like frills.

This boy cannot breathe in water.
He wears an air tank while he dives.
He breathes air through a set of tubes
and wears a mask to protect his eyes.

air tubes

air tank
on back

mask

Air and our senses

We have five senses, did you know?

They are sight, hearing, smell, taste, and touch.

Air helps us smell, see, and hear.

Without it we could not sense much.

How can you tell if foods taste good?

Can you tell by how they look and smell?

How do you know if a skunk is nearby?

Does it come and ring your doorbell?

Does a skunk smell sweet like a rose,

or does it make you plug your nose?

Sound waves move through water and air.
Some sounds, like sirens, warn us to beware.
We hear sounds around us with our ears,
like music and this girl yelling cheers.
The girl below is playing a song.
The boy above hears it and sings along.
Which other senses do they use?
Can you guess,
or do you need some clues?

Yeah, cheers!

All around our bodies,
there is warm or cold air.
It touches our skin and
blows through our hair.

13

Air and plants

Plants use air in a different way.
They take in carbon dioxide
and send oxygen away.
They combine carbon dioxide
with sunlight and water, too,
to make food for themselves
and for me and you.

Plants give off oxygen while making food.
They make the air fresh, clean, and renewed.
The kinds of plants that make the air clean
are the plants which have leaves that are green.

oxygen

carbon dioxide

water

Planting trees helps clean the air.
Can you plant some trees
to show that you care?
The oxygen they make
is for living things to share.

When you eat foods that are locally grown,
less gas is used to drive them to your home.
Local foods are healthier for you,
*and less gas means less air **pollution**, too.*

Using air

Air has no shape of its own,

but it gives shapes to objects

like the ones that are shown.

Which ones needed to be blown?

Which ones are able to be thrown?

Which ones can bounce up and down?

Which ones were made by a clown?

Without air,
this boat could not float.
The balloon in the sky could not fly.
Without air,
you could not bounce a ball,
nor ride your bike very far at all.
And if you tried blowing a bubble,
you would have a lot of trouble!

What kind of wind?

Wind is air moving over the ground.

It can move fast or slow.

Wind can be warm, or it can be cold.

Wind can blow rain, sleet, or snow.

*A gentle **breeze** blows the flags above. It is the kind of wind we love.*

*A **gale** is a very strong wind that blows. It may blow off some of these children's clothes!*

Hurricane winds gather over warm seas and destroy buildings and trees on land.
A **haboob** is a strong desert wind that carries soil, dirt, or sand.
A **monsoon** can be wet or dry with flood waters that rise very high.
A **tornado's** spinning winds are the worst of all.
They cause objects in their path to fall.

hurricane

hurricane from above

tornado

monsoon

The argon dance

There is a gas in air called **argon**
that doesn't change or go away.
The argon that dinosaurs breathed out
is a part of your breath today.
Argon connects us with the past
and with the future, too.
Whatever will live many years from now
will breathe the air you now do.
Follow the argon dance shown here
and see how it connects us far and near.

*Part of every breath you take
has been breathed by someone before.
Argon is shared by you and me,
as well as so many more!
This dinosaur breathed argon
millions of years ago.
The argon then continued to flow
around the world
in strong winds that blow.*

*The argon dance is not just on land.
It also takes place at sea.
When this dolphin leaps up to take a breath,
it inhales argon exhaled by me.*

The argon dance keeps on going
in every place and time.
These **pioneer** kids
did the argon dance
while reciting a happy rhyme.
The children lived 200 years ago,
but the argon they breathed
still continues to flow.

Children today do the argon dance
in many countries and places.
They are happy to be connected by air.
You can tell by their smiling faces.

Match them up!

1. Which of these things can be seen in the sky?
2. Which are the ones that cannot fly?
3. Which of these things are flying with wings?
4. Which of these things fly with wires or strings?

A. *hot-air balloon*

B. *butterfly*

Ⓒ airplane

Ⓓ balloons

Ⓔ eagle (bird)

Ⓕ hang glider

Ⓖ child

Ⓗ kite

Ⓘ sailboat

Ⓙ dog

Answers

1. A, B, C, D, E, F, H
2. G, I, J
3. B, C, E, F
4. A, D, F, H

23

Glossary

Note: Some boldfaced words are defined where they appear in the book.

blood cell A cell in the blood that delivers oxygen to body parts

carbon dioxide A gas found in air that plants use to make food

dew Water in the air that forms drops on things that are cool

exhale To breathe out

gas A part of air, such as oxygen

inhale To breathe in

lungs The organs that humans and many animals use to breathe

monsoon A strong wind that brings heavy rains or dry weather

organ A body part, such as a lung, which does an important job

oxygen A gas in the air that humans and animals need to breathe

pioneer One of the first people to settle in an area

pollution Something that dirties the air or the land

sound wave The movement of sound through air, water, or other substances

tornado A violent funnel-shaped wind

water vapor Tiny droplets of water found in air

Index

24